M257 Unit 2
UNDERGRADUATE COMPUTING

Putting Java to work

Java in the small

Unit 2

This publication forms part of an Open University course M257 *Putting Java to work*. Details of this and other Open University courses can be obtained from the Student Registration and Enquiry Service, The Open University, PO Box 197, Milton Keynes MK7 6BJ, United Kingdom: tel. +44 (0)870 333 4340, email general-enquiries@open.ac.uk

Alternatively, you may visit the Open University website at http://www.open.ac.uk where you can learn more about the wide range of courses and packs offered at all levels by The Open University.

To purchase a selection of Open University course materials visit http://www.ouw.co.uk, or contact Open University Worldwide, Michael Young Building, Walton Hall, Milton Keynes MK7 6AA, United Kingdom for a brochure. tel. +44 (0)1908 858785; fax +44 (0)1908 858787; email ouwenq@open.ac.uk

The Open University
Walton Hall, Milton Keynes
MK7 6AA

First published 2007. Second edition 2008.

Edited, designed and typeset by The Open University.

Printed and bound in the United Kingdom by Hobbs the Printers Ltd.

ISBN 978 0 7492 6797 1

2.1

The paper used in this publication contains pulp sourced from forests independently certified to the Forest Stewardship Council® (FSC®) principles and criteria. Chain of custody certification allows the pulp from these forests to be tracked to the end use (see www.fsc-uk.org).

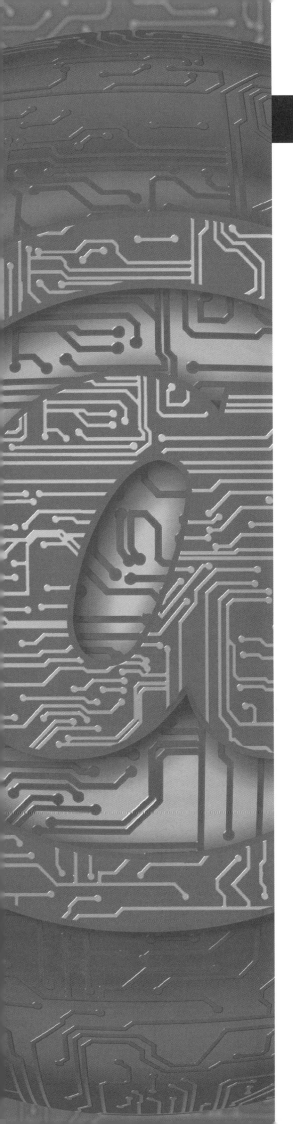

CONTENTS

M257 COURSE TEAM

M257 *Putting Java to work* was adapted from M254 *Java everywhere*.

M254 was produced by the following team.

Martin Smith, Course Team Chair and Author

Anton Dil, Author

Brendan Quinn, Author

Janet Van der Linden, Academic Editor

Barbara Poniatowska, Course Manager

Ralph Greenwell, Course Manager

Alkis Stavrinides, External Assessor, Coventry University

Critical readers

Pauline Curtis, Associate Lecturer

David Knowles, Associate Lecturer

Robin Walker, Associate Lecturer

Richard Walker, Associate Lecturer

The M257 adaptation was produced by:

Darrel Ince, Course Team Chair and Author

Richard Walker, Consultant Author and Critical Reader

Matthew Nelson, Critical Reader

Barbara Poniatowska, Course Manager

Ralph Greenwell, Course Manager

Alkis Stavrinides, External Assessor, Coventry University

Media development staff

Andrew Seddon, Media Project Manager

Ian Blackham, Editor

Anna Edgley-Smith, Editor

Jenny Brown, Freelance Editor

Andrew Whitehead, Designer and Graphic Artist

Glen Derby, Designer

Phillip Howe, Compositor

Lisa Hale, Compositor

Thanks are due to the Desktop Publishing Unit of the Faculty of Mathematics and Computing.

1 Introduction

We have called this unit 'Java in the small' after a term coined by DeRemer and Kron in a 1976 paper. This refers to the programming of the internal parts of programs, in particular the contents of methods.

DeRemer, F. and Kron, H. H. (1976) 'Programming-in-the-Large versus Programming-in-the-Small', *IEEE Transactions on Software Engineering*, vol. 2, no. 2, pp. 80–6.

The previous unit introduced the idea of objects communicating through the invocation of methods on objects. In this unit you will learn:

► how to write the internal parts of methods;

► the different types of data that the language provides;

► the facilities for altering the flow of program execution.

Our discussion is still within the framework that we adopted in the previous unit. The code we show here is assumed to be embedded in methods that access, and sometimes modify, instance variables. Methods are in turn contained in classes, which we discuss in detail in *Unit 3*.

Our objective is to create code that will be easy to read (whether by the original writer or somebody else), as well as easy to maintain. Of course, it must also be correct!

2 Data types

We begin our discussion of the main features of Java by talking about the various kinds of data that you can create and manipulate in Java programs.

2.1 Strong typing

Data can be created and manipulated in Java programs using variables (in which we can store and access data, as you saw in *Unit 1*) and **expressions** (for example, 2 + 3 is an arithmetic expression). Java is a **strongly typed** language, which means that every variable and expression has a type when the program is compiled and that you cannot arbitrarily assign values of one type to another.

There are two categories of type in Java: **primitive types** and **reference types**. We can create primitive variables and reference variables. Primitive variables store data values. Reference variables do not themselves store data values, but are used to refer to objects.

Reference variables are discussed in detail in *Unit 3*.

There are many kinds of primitive types and reference types. In fact, you can create your own reference types, as we shall see in the next unit, meaning that there is no limit to the number of these. There is a fixed set of primitive types; these are detailed next.

2.2 Primitive data types

Java (like most languages) has a number of primitive data types:

▶ numeric types to represent integers within various ranges;

▶ numeric types to represent non-integer numbers;

▶ a character type;

▶ a logical type.

Associated with every primitive type is a set of **literal** values. For example, the character 4 in a program is a literal value of the type known as `int` (a type used to store integers). Literals have fixed values. The character 4 always means the same thing. In contrast, a variable can contain different values at different times, so its meaning is not fixed.

One way of storing a value in a variable is by assigning a literal value to the variable. For example, we could write:

```
int newVal = 4;
```

Declaration and initialization

In *Unit 1* we discussed how we can reserve memory locations for storing values of any primitive type. Those memory locations can then be made to contain values that are legal for the particular type. This involves two steps.

1   Create a variable of the type you want to use. This step is called **declaration** or declaring a variable.

2   When you first store something useful in a variable's memory location, we call it **initialization** or initializing a variable.

Integral types

The integral types are called `byte`, `short`, `int` and `long`. All of these types are said to be signed, meaning that they can hold positive or negative numbers. Each has a different capacity. For example, a `byte` can store any number between –128 and 127, whereas a `short` can store a number between –32768 and 32767.

In general, you should pick the type that occupies the least memory and meets your needs for the range of numbers you wish to store. However, for convenience, we will use `int` whenever we want to deal with integers.

Integer literals are of type `int`, and so are compatible with `int` type variables.

To declare two variables of type `int` and initialize them we write:

```
int myInt;
int myOtherInt;
myInt = 888;
myOtherInt = -2;
```

The last two statements store the value 888 in the memory reserved for `myInt` and the value –2 in the memory reserved for `myOtherInt`.

We can change the value stored by writing another assignment statement, for example:

```
myInt = 777;
```

or we can assign one identifier to another as follows:

```
myInt = myOtherInt;
```

This will copy the contents of the memory location whose name is `myOtherInt` into the memory location whose name is `myInt`.

The `char` type

Java has a character data type called `char`, which allows you to represent single characters. Character literals are denoted by a value enclosed within single quotes:

```
char alpha;
char punc;
char num;
alpha = 'e';
punc = '?';
num = '1';
```

The above statements declare and initialize three character variables, `alpha`, `punc` and `num`. The variable `alpha` has been initialized to contain the character `'e'`, `punc` has been initialized to contain the character `'?'`, while `num` has the value `'1'`, which is not the same as the integer value 1.

A character variable can be assigned any value in the **Unicode** character set, which is an international set of characters (for example, Greek and French characters such as `'Δ'` and `'é'` are included). This means that we can write software for users around the world.

Escape sequences

The character literal `'\u00A9'` is an example of an **escape sequence**, which is a sequence of characters standing in place of a single value. Escape sequences in Java are marked by the use of the backslash character, which indicates that what follows is not to be interpreted literally. The characters following the backslash indicate the nature of the special information being represented. In this case, `u00A9` indicated that this was the Unicode character with value 00A9. Character literals allow us to specify non-standard characters such as ©.

Data type sizes in Java are fixed to ensure portability across implementations of the language.

Unicode characters may not display correctly when using console output.

The newline character is not the same as the line separator on various platforms.

Some other examples of escape sequences relate to characters that are not printable; for example, the 'tab' horizontal spacing character has no obvious literal representation.

The most commonly used escape sequence is the character '\n', in which the n stands for 'newline', meaning the character that moves the screen cursor down one line. '\\' is the literal for the backslash character.

The literal for the single quote character is '\'', in which there are two single quotes after the backslash, the second of which indicates the end of the literal.

Floating-point types

In order to represent numbers that may include fractional parts, we use **floating-point types**.

You will be familiar with this idea if you have come across scientific notation. In this notation, the speed of light in a vacuum is approximately 2.998×10^8 metres per second. The two parts of the number are its digits, 2.998, and a multiplying factor, 10^8, which tells us about the magnitude.

The floating-point representation gives rise to the name of one of these types, which is float. The other floating-point type is called double (which is short for 'double precision'). The float type has 32 bits of space and double has 64 bits.

Thus the statement:

```
double cashValue = 23.8;
```

declares a double precision variable cashValue and initializes it to 23.8, which is a literal floating-point value.

Floating-point literals are denoted either by writing them as *integerpart.fractionalpart*, as we did above, or by using scientific notation, where the character e or E denotes the fact that the number is to be multiplied by the power of ten of the integer following the e or E. So, if we wanted to write the value for the speed of light we used above, we might have said:

```
double speedOfLight = 2.998e8;
```

The type of the floating-point literal we have shown is double.

There is just one primitive type left, the logical type boolean, which is the simplest of the primitive types! We shall discuss this type in Subsection 5.1. Before that, we shall look at how we can make use of the types we have already discussed.

SAQ 1

(a) List the primitive types in Java.

(b) Why is Unicode important for Java's portability?

ANSWERS ....

(a) They are byte, short, int, long, float, double, boolean and char.

(b) Unicode provides an international character set, which allows us to write software usable in various parts of the world.

SAQ 2

Which of the following attempts to create initialized variables would cause a compilation error?

(a) `int j = 1.2;`

(b) `int k = -200;`

(c) `int ok = 1;`

(d) `int boolean = 1;`

(e) `char myChar = '\n';`

(f) `char c = -10;`

(g) `char e = 'e';`

(h) `char d = '\';`

ANSWERS ....

The following produce compilation errors:

(a) the literal `1.2` is not an integer;

(d) the variable name `boolean` is not allowed, because it is a keyword;

(f) the literal `-10` is not a `char`;

(h) the literal `'\'` is badly formed; for a backslash it should be `'\\'`;

2.3 Casting

Primitive variables can store values only of the type they are declared to be. However, there are occasions where we want to be able to convert from one type to another. Sometimes types can be converted automatically, but when we have to specify a type conversion it is known as **casting**.

Casting involves writing the desired type of an expression in parentheses in front of the expression; for example, we would write `(int)` in front of an expression if we wanted it to be converted to an `int`.

The full rules of type conversion are lengthy and we do not want you to learn them. The following discussion aims to give you only the general idea of how casting operates. The most important thing to bear in mind is that casting primitive types can result in loss of information and therefore you must think carefully before casting to decide if this is acceptable.

A need to cast may be a sign that your choice of types is wrong.

Casting and information loss

Only variables of the floating-point types can store information about fractional parts of numbers. The fractional parts are lost if casting to an integral type.

It is possible to convert one integral type to another or one floating-point type to another; however, because variables of different types occupy different amounts of memory, this can cause information loss.

Some examples are given below.

Example 1

Bearing in mind that the value 35 is a literal of type int, the following shows casting an int to a byte:

```
byte b = (byte) 35;
```

This results in b storing the value 35.

Example 2

This example shows casting of a double to an int:

```
double doubVal;
int intVal;
doubVal = 2.8;
intVal = (int) doubVal; // casting to an int
```

Here the value in doubVal is cast to an int type, and the converted value is then assigned to intVal, so that intVal is given the value of the integer part of doubVal.

After the conversion, intVal will contain the value 2. The fractional part of the data has been lost. (The contents of the variable doubVal are unchanged by this operation.)

Example 3

It is possible to convert integers to the char type, because the underlying type of char is integral:

```
int a = 35, b = 12, d = 13;
char c;
c = (char) (a + b + d);
```

This results in c being assigned the value 60, which is the 61st character in the Unicode set (the first being character zero). This turns out to be the character '<'.

When is a cast required?

A cast is always required to convert a floating-point type to an integral type. In other cases, a cast is required if the type you are assigning (on the right-hand side of an equals sign) occupies a larger space in memory than the type you are assigning to (on the left-hand side of an equals sign). When a cast is required, the resulting value is not necessarily the same as the value the cast is applied to.

If you have not specified a cast in a case where a cast is required, the compiler will produce a compilation error with the message that there is a 'possible loss of precision'.

What would happen if we were to assign an `int` variable to a `double`?

```
double doubVal;
int intVal;
intVal = 2;
doubVal = (double) intVal;   // this is allowed
doubVal = intVal;            // this is also allowed!
```

Although you can write a cast to convert an `int` to a `double`, Java does not require you to do so. This is because an `int` occupies 32 bits, and a `double` occupies 64 bits. There is no danger that we lose information in converting the `int` to a `double`.

Because this type conversion would not result in information loss, Java does not require you to write a cast, and will perform the conversion automatically. This is known as **promotion**. After each assignment above, `doubVal` would contain the value `2.0`.

3 Statements, scope and operators

In this section we discuss in what parts of our code it is legal to use a declared variable, which depends on what is known as the scope of a declaration. We also look at operations we can perform on the data in our programs. To do this, we first need to define what we mean by a line of code, or a statement.

3.1 Statements and scope

A **statement** is a unit of executable code, usually terminated by a semicolon.

Statements can be written to occupy one line of code, but the physical layout of code is not significant, and it is possible to have a single statement that extends over several lines of code.

Groups of statements in Java can be treated as a **code block** by enclosing them in curly brackets. For example, the code fragment:

It is easy to forget to type the closing curly bracket. A good programming discipline is to start with a pair of brackets and then fill in their contents. Your IDE may do this for you.

```
{
    int i;
    int j = 24;
    i = j;
}
```

is an example of a code block consisting of three statements. The statements in a block are executed in order from top to bottom.

A code block enables a set of statements to be treated as a single statement.

Although in some cases it is legal, you should avoid declaring a variable identifier both inside and outside a code block.

Variables declared inside a code block are valid only inside the brackets. We say that the variables' **scope** is the region enclosed by the brackets and we call them **local variables**. For example, i and j above are local variables and are valid only within the curly brackets.

You can nest code blocks, as shown below:

```
{
    int k; // k valid from here
    {
        // k is valid, so this is okay
        int j = k;
        // j valid until next closing curly bracket
    }
    // j no longer valid, k still valid
}
```

Here variable k's scope includes the inner curly brackets.

3.2 Primitive operators

All the primitive data types that are provided in Java are associated with sets of **operators**. For example, integers and floating-point types have addition and subtraction operators. Operators can have single arguments, in which case they are known as unary operators; they can also have two arguments, in which case they are known as binary operators.

There are rules that determine the type of every expression and we can assign an expression to a variable of the same type. In this way, we can save the result of operations we have performed.

Operations involving variables will be meaningful only if the variables have been properly initialized, so it is good practice to give any variables you declare an initial value.

Arithmetic operators

Arithmetic operators are used with floating-point numbers and the various integral types. All the standard arithmetic operations are available, as Table 1 shows.

Table 1 Arithmetic operators

Operator	Name	Example expression	Meaning
*	Multiplication	a * b	a times b
/	Division	a / b	a divided by b
%	Remainder (modulus)	a % b	the remainder after dividing a by b
+	Addition	a + b	a plus b
−	Subtraction	a − b	a minus b

The type of an arithmetic expression depends on the type of its arguments. For example, 3.0/4.0 is 0.75, but the result of 3/4 is 0. In the second case, because the arguments are integers, the operator does an integer division and discards the fractional part of the result.

Similarly, 15/2 evaluates to 7, because the fractional part is discarded, but 15/2.0 evaluates to 7.5, because if either argument is a floating-point number, the result is a floating-point number.

The modulus operator returns the value that is the remainder when its left argument is divided by its right argument. For example, the value of 34%5 is 4, since this is the remainder when 34 is divided by 5. If either argument is a floating-point number, the result is also a floating-point number. For example, the value of 3.5%2.1 is 1.4, because 2.1 'goes into' 3.5 once, with a remainder of 1.4.

34 % 5 may be read as '34 mod 5'.

The negation operator

A unary operator ('unary' means it has only one argument) that you might wish to use at some point is the negation operator. An example is as follows:

```
int a = 2;
int b = -a;
```

This has the effect of setting b to the value −2. The single argument for the negation operator appears to the right of the minus sign. We say that this is a **prefix** operator, which simply means that it appears before the value it takes as an argument.

The compiler is able to distinguish the subtraction operator from the negation operator by the number of arguments it has.

Precedence of arithmetic operators

So far we have seen only simple arithmetic expressions. What if we were to write 3 + 4 * 5? How does the compiler interpret this? Does it mean add three to four and then multiply by five (to give 35)? Or does it mean multiply four by five, then add three (to give 23)?

Each programming language has its own precedence rules.

If an expression involves more than one operator, there is a clear order in which operators are evaluated, determined by what is known as **operator precedence**. The answer to the expression 3 + 4 * 5 is 23, not 35, because multiplication has a higher precedence than addition, which means it is done first.

We are deliberately not stating the precedence rules. Instead, you should ensure a clear order of evaluation of an expression, using parentheses. Java will evaluate expressions in parentheses first.

If you write 3 + (4 * 5), this means first evaluate four times five and then add three. Anyone reading your code can tell this without remembering the precedence of operators.

If you write (3 + 4) * 5, it is equally clear you mean to add three and four before multiplying by five.

Increment and decrement operators

Two operators you will find yourself using frequently in Java are the increment and decrement operators, ++ and − −. These have two forms: **postfix** and prefix. The ++ operator increments the variable it is associated with by 1 and the − − operator decrements the value of the variable it is associated with by 1. Suppose we have:

```
int myInt = 0;
myInt++;      // postfix increment
++myInt;      // prefix increment
```

After the first increment myInt has the value 1 and after the second it has the value 2. In this context, there is no difference between the prefix and postfix operators.

However, the increment and decrement operations return values that can be used in any context where their type is valid, and this is where these operators differ. The postfix variant (in which the operator appears after the argument) returns the *old* value of the variable to which it is applied whereas the prefix form returns the *new* value.

For example, consider:

```
int myInt = 10;
int x = myInt++; // postfix form
```

The second statement increments the value of the variable myInt and places this value back into myInt. It then returns the *old* value of myInt and this is stored in x. After this code, myInt would have the value 11 and x would have the value 10.

However, it would be different if we had written:

```
int myInt = 10;
int x = ++myInt; // prefix form
```

After this code, both `x` and `myInt` would have the value `11`, since the prefix increment operator returns the value of `myInt` *after* it is incremented.

The action of the `--` operators is the same, except that subtraction rather than addition occurs.

The properties of the `++` and `--` operators are summarized in Table 2.

Table 2 Increment and decrement operators

Operator	Name	Example expression	Meaning
++	Postfix increment	x++	add 1 to x and return the old value
++	Prefix increment	++x	add 1 to x and return the new value
--	Postfix decrement	x--	take 1 from x and return the old value
--	Prefix decrement	--x	take 1 from x and return the new value

SAQ 3

Give the values of the following expressions or indicate if there is an error:

(a) `1 + (2 * 3)`   (f) `2 % 3`

(b) `(1 + 2) * 3`   (g) `5 / 2`

(c) `6 % 2`   (h) `5 / 0`

(d) `17 % 12`   (i) `0 / 5`

(e) `5 % 0`   (j) `5 / 2.0`

ANSWERS ....

(a) 7

(b) 9

(c) 0 (2 goes into 6 three times, with no remainder).

(d) 5

(e) This would cause a run-time error, due to division by zero. (Our compiler does not catch this.)

(f) 2 (3 goes into 2 zero times and leaves a remainder of 2).

(g) 2 (the answer is truncated to an integer).

(h) Run-time error, due to division by zero. (Our compiler does not catch this.)

(i) 0

(j) 2.5 (because at least one argument is floating-point, the result is floating-point).

Activity 2.1
Experimenting with data types and operators.

4 Strings

In this section we begin our discussion of another commonly used type, the string. A **string** is a sequence of characters. For example, a string could be used to store a person's name. In Java, strings are represented using the reference type called `String`.

String declaration

Strings and other reference types can be declared in the same way as primitive data types such as `int` and `char`, by stating the type and then the names of the variables. The code:

```
String name, address;
```

declares two variables of type `String`. No strings are created by such a declaration and the reference values in these variables have not yet been initialized.

String creation

String literals are denoted by enclosing their characters in double quotation marks. The text `"David Jones"` is an example of a `String` literal. Thus, the statements:

```
String name;           // declare
name = "David Jones";  // initialize
```

declare the variable `name`, of type `String`, and initialize that variable to contain a reference to the `String` object storing the characters `"David Jones"`.

A special `String` literal is the string with no contents, called the **empty string** (written `""`). We can write:

```
name = "";
```

Such an assignment does not (of itself) destroy the `"David Jones"` string or alter it; rather it creates a new string and makes our `name` variable reference the new string. It is possible that some other string variable could continue to reference `"David Jones"`. Any character can appear in a `String`, including the escape sequences. The double quotation mark can be used as follows:

```
\ "
```

This enables the programmer to write strings that contain double quotation marks, for example the string `"This is a double quotation mark \ ""`.

Example 4

To illustrate these points, consider the following segments of code and the related figures:

```
String name, name2;    // Figure 1
name = "David Jones";  // Figure 2
name2 = name;          // Figure 3
name = "Roderick";     // Figure 4
```

In *Unit 1* we used a rectangle to depict a primitive variable's memory location. Here, in Figure 1, we have used a circle to depict a reference variable. After the first line of code, we have created two reference variables, with the given names.

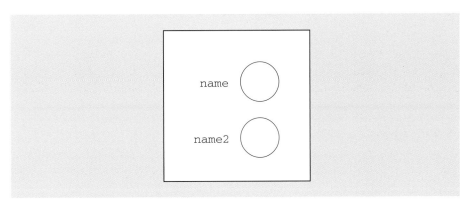

Figure 1   Two uninitialized reference variables

After the second line of code, we have created a `String` object containing the text `"David Jones"` and have made the `name` variable reference that string (see Figure 2). We have shown the reference as an arrow linking a reference variable to a memory location.

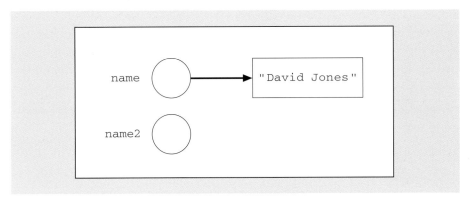

Figure 2   The **name** variable referencing a **String** object

The effect of the next assignment is to copy the reference held in `name` to `name2`. This results in `name2` referencing the same memory location as `name`, as shown in Figure 3.

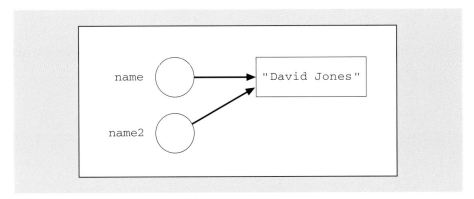

Figure 3   Two variables referencing the same object

By assignment of a new string literal, we can make `name` reference a new memory location, as shown in Figure 4. The amount of memory set aside in each case to store the actual string data depends on the length of the string.

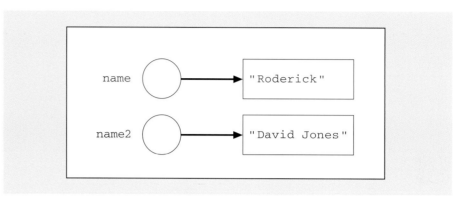

Figure 4   The **name** variable referencing a new object

The `length` method

You can invoke a `length` method on a `String` object in order to find out its length. For example, the expression:

```
name.length()
```

evaluates to the number of characters in the string referenced by `name`. If this string were `"Roderick"`, the `length` method would return the value 8. The empty string has length zero.

String concatenation

Because we often want to print strings on our computer screens, the operator that joins (concatenates) strings is frequently used. This is the concatenation operator, written +.

The arithmetic + operator is distinguished by the type of its arguments.

If either of its arguments is a `String`, the + operator will automatically turn any arguments into strings before carrying out a concatenation operation.

For example, we can write the following:

```
int occupants = 2;
String address = "Filby Lane";
String printout;
printout = address + " has " + occupants + " occupants";
```

The right-hand side of the assignment would convert `occupants` to a string and then concatenate all the strings to create the single string `"Filby Lane has 2 occupants"`. By assignment, the `printout` variable would then be made to reference that string object.

SAQ 4

Complete the following class so that it produces the output "Juma P Jambo was 8 years old." The line System.out.println will display its string argument on your computer.

```
public class Concatenate
{
    public static void main (String args [])
    {
        // add some variables here
        // age has value 8
        // initial has value 'P'
        // firstName references "Juma"
        // lastName references "Jambo"
        System.out.println(firstName + /* etc */);
    }
}
```

ANSWER...

```
    public class Concatenate
    {
        public static void main (String args [])
        {
            int age = 8;
            char initial = 'P';
            String firstName = "Juma";
            String lastName = "Jambo";
            System.out.println(firstName + " " + initial +
                " " + lastName + " was " + age + " years old.");
        }
    }
```

You could use other variable names, but they should be reflected in the println statement. Notice that we had to add blank spaces so that the text is correctly spaced.

Activity 2.2
Experimenting with strings and concatenation.

5 Conditional processing

Any useful program must be able to respond to changes in the data on which it operates. For example:

▶ if a member of staff is a manager, his or her salary will be calculated using a productivity bonus;

▶ if the stock of a particular product in a warehouse is empty, then the sales clerk will be informed that the order cannot be met;

▶ if the satellite has not emitted a signal for over 30 minutes, the main controller will be alerted.

The **flow control structures** determine the way in which a Java program is executed, allowing different segments of code to be executed under different circumstances.

In this section we describe the control structures in Java that enable conditional processing, and put them to use in small code fragments and in methods. First, we must describe two other fundamental features of the language: the `boolean` type, and relational operators.

5.1   The `boolean` type

We deferred discussion of this last remaining primitive type from Section 2.

Variables of the `boolean` type can hold either the literal value `true` or the literal value `false`, which are keywords in the Java language. This allows us to express conditions such as those suggested above and determine whether they are true or false. For example, we can write:

```
boolean dog = true;
boolean doberman = false;
```

We will call an expression that evaluates to a `boolean` value a **logical expression**.

Java defines a number of relational operators for boolean types.

5.2   Relational operators

The **relational operators** tell you about relationships between values of the same type. Their arguments can be integers, floating-point numbers, or characters. The 'equal to' and 'not equal to' operators can also be used with the `boolean` type.

The operators are summarized in Table 3. Notice especially that the equality operator is two equals signs, one after the other. It is easy to forget to type one of these signs, which changes the meaning of the expression to an assignment.

Table 3 Relational operators and expressions

Operator	Name	Example expression	Meaning
==	Equal to	x == y	true if x equals y, otherwise false
!=	Not equal to	x != y	true if x is not equal to y, otherwise false
>	Greater than	x > y	true if x is greater than y, otherwise false
<	Less than	x < y	true if x is less than y, otherwise false
>=	Greater than or equal to	x >= y	true if x is greater than or equal to y, otherwise false
<=	Less than or equal to	x <= y	true if x is less than or equal to y, otherwise false

An expression involving a relational operator is a logical expression, so has a `boolean` value.

The following expressions would all evaluate to `true`:

```
1 < 2
0.5 > 0.0
true != false
false == false
2 == 2
'a' < 'c'
```

Arguments of relational operators can also be expressions. For example, if the values of the variables a, b and c were 34, 56 and 3 respectively, then the value of:

```
(a + b) < c
```

would be `false` and the value of the expression below would be `true`:

```
(a + 81) == ((b * 2) + c)
```

Take care when using relational operators with floating-point values: we can only store such values approximately, and this can lead to surprising results.

SAQ 5

Which of the following combined declarations and initializations are incorrect, and why?

(a) `boolean bob = 0;`

(b) `boolean sue = TRUE;`

(c) `boolean f = false;`

ANSWERS ....

(a) Incorrect, the literal 0 is not `boolean`.

(b) Incorrect, the literal `TRUE` is not `boolean`, because Java is case-sensitive.

(c) This is syntactically correct.

SAQ 6

Explain why each of the following expressions is syntactically incorrect, assuming the following declarations have been made:

```
boolean g = false, h = false;
int a = 1, b = 1;
```

(a) `a > g`

(b) `g == 0`

(c) `h == True`

(d) `g < h`

ANSWERS ....

(a) `a` and `g` are of different types and no promotion can occur to make the types compatible. (It is not legal to cast between the `boolean` type and any other types.)

(b) `g` and `0` are not the same type and no promotion can occur to make the types compatible.

(c) `True` is not a `boolean` value (`true` is).

(d) The `<` operator is not defined for boolean arguments.

5.3   The `if` statement

We are now in a position to return to the subject of the Java flow control structures for conditional processing, also known as **selection statements**. Selection statements give us ways of specifying the conditions for changing the flow of control in a program. The general form of our first conditional processing statement is shown below:

```
if (logical_expression)
{
    statements;
}
```

Here, if the `logical_expression` within the parentheses evaluates to `true`, then any `statements` in the following code block are executed. We often refer to the code block as the **body** of the `if` statement.

If the `logical_expression` is `false`, then any `statements` in the body of the `if` statement are not executed.

Two examples of simple `if` statements are shown below:

```
if (a == 12)
{
    b = 23;
}
if (c > 123)
{
    signal = true;
}
```

▶ The first statement sets the integer variable `b` to `23` if the current value of the integer variable `a` is `12`.

▶ The second statement sets the `boolean` variable `signal` to be `true` if the value of the integer variable `c` is greater than `123`.

An `if` statement may cover several lines of code, but it is just one statement. As is usual when a statement has a body in curly brackets, there is no semicolon at its end.

It is permitted, syntactically, to omit curly brackets when there is only one statement in the body of the `if` statement. So we could also have written:

```
if (a == 12)
    b = 23;
if (c > 123)
    signal = true;
```

In this case, each semicolon above terminates a statement. However, it is better style to use curly brackets, to demarcate clearly the body of the `if` statement.

We can have as many statements as we require in the body of an `if` statement, written as a code block. For example:

```
if (a == b)
{
    b = 23;
    signal = true;
    a = 0;
}
```

Here, the three variables `b`, `signal` and `a` are given values if the integer variable `a` has the same value as the integer variable `b`.

We have adopted a style of writing Java programs that includes indentation to indicate the structure of a program. Indentation aids readability of code, but does not affect the way the compiler interprets it.

5.4 Variables of type **boolean** and **if** statements

A `boolean` variable is used when we want to store information about the truth or falsity of some part of our program. As an example of this consider the following.

```
int fish;
boolean caughtFish;
fish = 10;
caughtFish = (fish > 0);
```

This would result in `caughtFish` being set to `true`. Thereafter we could use `caughtFish` in code where we need to test this condition.

We can now write statements such as this:

```
if (caughtFish)
{
    // do something
}
```

Suppose that we had to use this condition several times, and that we had repeatedly written fish > 0; we would have to locate and change each of those lines if the condition were changed to fish > 1. Storing the condition in a boolean variable has the advantage that we would have to change its meaning in only one place: where we assigned a value to caughtFish. That line would now change to:

```
caughtFish = (fish > 1);
```

No other changes to our code would be required.

SAQ 7

Write code to do the following, assuming the declarations below have been made:

```
int a, b;
```

(a) Set a to the value 1 if b is less than or equal to 2.

(b) Increment b by 1 if b is greater than 5.

ANSWERS ....

(a)

```
if (b <= 2)
{
    a = 1;
}
```

(b)

```
if (b > 5)
{

    b++;

}
```

5.5   The if ... else statement

There is a slightly more complicated form of the if statement that allows you to specify code to be processed when the logical condition is false in addition to code to be processed when it is true.

The general form of this statement is:

Note that there is no semicolon between the code blocks here.

```
if (logical_expression)
{
    statementsA;
}
else
{
    statementsB;
}
```

where statementsA are executed if the logical_expression is true and statementsB are executed if the expression is false.

An example might be that if a user has indicated he is a novice we set our user interface to its verbose mode; otherwise we set it to normal mode. We could write:

```
boolean novice, verbose;
// novice gets set to true or false
if (novice)
{
    verbose = true;
}
else
{
    verbose = false;
}
```

5.6 Nesting `if` statements

We can write `if` statements within `if` statements, which we call *nesting*. An example of this is shown below:

Nesting can occur within any of the Java conditional constructs.

```
if (a == 34)
{
    s = 23;
    i++;
    if (i < 23)
    {
        b++;
        c++;
    }
}
```

Here you can see the advantage of using an indentation style: the structure of the two `if` statements is displayed and it becomes clear which statements are going to be executed when either of the two logical expressions is true.

5.7 Logical operators

It is common to want to combine the results from several logical expressions. For example, we may want to allow a user to log in only if the username is recognized *and* the password is correct. Java provides logical operators, which roughly correspond to the natural language words 'and', 'or' and 'not', as a way of combining logical expressions.

The logical operators are summarized in Table 4. This shows the use of the arguments a and b.

Table 4 Logical operators and expressions

Operator	Name	Example expression	Meaning
`&&`	Logical AND	`a && b`	returns `true` if both a and b are `true`, otherwise `false`
`||`	Logical OR	`a || b`	returns `false` if both a and b are `false`, otherwise `true`
`!`	Logical NOT	`!a`	returns `false` if a is `true`; returns `true` if a is `false`

The arguments for a logical operator must be logical expressions.

As we have just seen, one way of forming a logical expression is using relational operators and variables with numeric types. It is possible for us to combine several conditions into one statement using the logical operators. For example, consider the code shown below:

```
int a, b;
boolean eitherPositive, bothNegative;
a = 22;
b = -33;
eitherPositive = (a > 0) || (b > 0);
bothNegative = (a < 0) && (b < 0);
```

The variable eitherPositive is assigned the value true, because a > 0 is true and therefore the whole expression is true (even though b > 0 is false). Only one part of an OR expression need be true for the whole expression to be true.

The variable bothNegative is assigned the value false because a < 0 is false, and therefore the whole expression is false. Even though b < 0 is true, this is not sufficient for the AND expression to be true.

SAQ 8

Assuming the following declarations:

```
int a = 1, b = 2;
```

write code to do the following:

(a) If a and b are equal print the text "equal", otherwise print the text "not equal".

(b) If a is greater than b, assign b the value of a; otherwise assign a the value of b.

(c) If a is greater than b, assign b the value of a; if b is greater than a, assign a the value of b.

(d) If a is greater than b and b is less than zero, assign b the value 1.

ANSWERS ....

(a) We could have a statement like the following:

```
if (a == b)
{
    System.out.println("equal");
}
else
{
    System.out.println("not equal");
}
```

(b) The following would achieve what we require:

```
if (a > b)
{
    b = a;
}
else
{
    a = b;
}
```

An alternative answer would be:

```
if (a <= b)
{
    a = b;
}
else
{
    b = a;
}
```

(c) We shall need something like the following:

```
if (a > b)
{
    b = a;
}
else
{
    if (b > a)
    {
        a = b;
    }
}
```

Note that this is different from the previous answer, because a is not assigned the value of b when a == b.

(d) We can use a single condition combining both requirements, using the logical AND operator:

```
if ((a > b) && (b < 0))
{
    b = 1;
}
```

This could also be achieved by a nested if.

5.8 The `switch ... case` statement

The `if` statement is used frequently, but can become unwieldy where a large number of outcomes need to be tested. One case is where a variable takes on one of several different values and different code must be executed depending on the value.

The `switch` statement makes this 'multiconditional branching' more readable. To use a switch, all cases must depend in the same way on the argument (in terms of logical equality).

The general format of the switch statement is:

A `break` statement transfers control to the end of its enclosing statement. Its form is simply the word `break` followed by a semicolon.

```
switch (argument)
{
    case selector:
        statements;
        break;
    case selector:
        statements;
        break;
    case selector:
        statements;
        break;
    // as many cases as required
    case selector:
        statements;
        break;
    default:
        statements;
        break;
}
```

The important points are:

▶   The *argument* is an expression of type `int`, `char`, `short` or `byte` (usually just the name of a variable).

▶   Each *selector* is a constant value (usually a literal) compatible with the *argument* type.

▶   A code block enclosing the statements in each case is optional but helps to demarcate the code for each case.

▶   The *statements* are performed if the case *selector* is logically equal to the *argument*; in other words, if *argument == selector*.

▶   The keyword to cause the switch to terminate is the word `break`. When the word `break` is encountered, control passes to the statement after the `switch` statement.

▶   A default case may be given to indicate processing to take place when no selector is matched.

It is a common error to forget that switch cases fall through.

Failure to use a `break` statement results in control 'falling through' to the next case, so that other statements are also executed. It is unusual to require this form of processing, so normal practice is to include a `break` statement at the end of every case. Many people consider the `switch` statement to be poorly designed for this reason.

An example of a `switch` statement whose argument is of type `char` is shown below:

```
char control;
// control is assigned a value
switch (control)
{
    case 'a':
    {
        videoId = 3;
        break;
    }
    case 'b':
    {
        videoId = 19;
        soundId = 12;
        break;
    }
    case 'c':
    {
        videoId = 11;
        link++;
        break;
    }
}
// after a break, or if no cases match,
// execution resumes here
```

Here the character variable `control` determines which statements are to be executed. If the value of this variable is the character `'a'` then the integer variable `videoId` is set to 3 and the `break` statement transfers control to the end of the `switch` statement, effectively transferring control to the statement following. If the value of the `control` variable is the character `'b'`, control is then passed to the three statements:

```
videoId = 19;
soundId = 12;
break;
```

After the first two statements have been executed, the `break` statement is invoked and, again, control is passed to the statement following the `switch` statement. The final part of the `switch` statement:

```
videoId = 11;
link++;
break;
```

is executed when the variable `control` contains the value `'c'`. The `break` statement again transfers control to the end of the `switch` statement.

If no cases are matched, control proceeds to the statement after the `switch` statement.

You may have deduced that the final `break` statement is strictly not necessary since, if it were omitted, the processing would pass to the end of the `switch` statement anyway. However, we regard it as good programming practice: you will often find that you will need to modify a program after it has been tested, and one common modification is to add new cases to a `switch` statement.

Suppose you added a new case to match value `'x'`, following the last case, and had not inserted a final `break`. Your code would look like this (we have omitted the optional curly brackets):

```
switch (control)
{
    case 'a':
        videoId = 3;
        break;
    case 'b':
        videoId = 19;
        soundId = 12;
        break;
    case 'c':
        videoId = 11;
        link++;
    case 'x' :
        // code for new case
}
```

When the processing for the case corresponding to the character `'c'` has completed, control will fall through to the new case that you have added, which is probably not what you intended. This sort of error is very difficult to detect. Thus, even though the final `break` may be unnecessary, it is good practice to include it: you could save yourself a large amount of development time.

SAQ 9

(a) When might you use a `switch` statement in preference to an `if` statement?

(b) Suggest why `float` is not a legal type of argument in a `switch` statement.

(c) What happens if you leave out a `break` statement at the end of a `case` statement's code block?

(d) What keyword do you use to specify code to be performed in a `switch` statement when no cases match the argument?

ANSWERS ....

(a) When you wish to test a variable (of a type compatible with `switch`) for equality with several different values and execute different code in each case.

(b) Floating-point types can only store numbers to a limited accuracy. This creates issues with tests for equality, on which a `switch` relies when choosing which case to perform.

(c) If that case is selected, the flow of control will proceed through its code block into the code block for the next case (or to the end of the `switch` statement, if the selected case is the last).

(d) You use the keyword `default` to specify a case to be performed in the event of no other cases matching.

Activity 2.3
Using `if` statements.

Activity 2.4
Understanding relational and logical operators.

6 Arrays

It is a common requirement when programming to have to process a collection of items of the same type. For example, one may have to add up a collection of numbers or check the due dates on a collection of library books.

It is convenient to be able to refer to such a collection as a group and to be able to **iterate** over the collection (that is, to process the items in the collection one at a time, re-using some code). Because this is such a common requirement, most languages provide a data structure, the array, to support this.

In this section you will learn how to create and access array structures in Java, and in the next section you will study the Java constructs for iteration.

Array indexing

An **array** is a collection of items of the same type. Figure 5 shows a simple array.

	0	1	2	3	4	5	6
	12	9	52	3	4	4	2

Figure 5   An array and its location indexes

As usual, we are depicting a primitive memory location as a rectangle. In showing these items side by side, we are indicating that they are part of a collection. They can be numbered as indicated above each box. We call this numbering an **index**.

This array contains seven values, all of which are integers. The first item in the array (at location zero) is 12, the second (at location 1) is 9, and so on.

In Java, the index that identifies the first value in an array is *zero* and the last is $n - 1$, where there are n items in the array.

In some other languages, array indexes start at 1.

Array declaration

In Java, array variables are references, not primitives. Because arrays are objects, they have instance variables we can access and we can invoke methods on them.

In many languages, arrays are a primitive type.

Already we have seen that integers can be declared by means of a statement such as:

```
int intValue;
```

An array can be declared using a similar syntax. For example, an array of integers could be declared as follows:

```
int [] holder;
```

The *type* of the array in this case is written `int []` and the array can contain only elements of the primitive type `int`. You can create an array of any primitive type; for example, other types of arrays of primitives are `boolean []`, `char []` and `double []`.

One may also write:

```
int holder [];
```

but this departs from the normal syntax of having the type appear at the beginning of the declaration, so we prefer to adopt the previous style.

Unit 3 says more about arrays whose contents are reference types.

One may also have an array of a reference type; for example, we could have an array of strings of type `String []`.

As with other reference types, declaration does not create an object of the type; it only creates a reference, in this case to an array type object.

Array initializers

Java provides a quick way of creating and initializing an array by assigning a list of initial values in curly brackets to an array type variable. For example, the declaration and assignment:

```
int [] holder = { 1, 1, 1, 1, 1};
```

An 'array initializer' is not a literal. Its main use is in an array initialization.

declares an integer array with five elements, with the initial value of these elements being 1. The expression on the right of the assignment sign is called an **array initializer**.

In creating an array you reserve enough memory for the collection of values in the array initializer.

This is obviously not a feasible way of creating very large arrays, because it relies on us listing all the elements by hand.

This is shown in Figure 6.

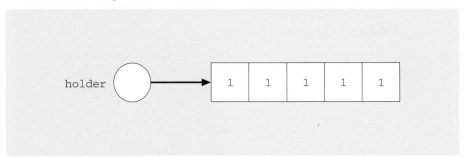

Figure 6　An array variable referencing an array

It would be illegal to write the following:

```
int [] holder2 = {false, true}
```

because the array initializer in this case is of type `boolean []`, while `holder2` is of type `int []`, and these types are not compatible.

6.1　Assigning values to individual elements

Since each memory location can be referred to by the index, each can be initialized individually. For example, to initialize (or change) the *fourth* element of the `firstLetters` array containing `'a'`, `'b'`, `'c'` and `'d'` to the value `'c'` (see Figure 7), we can write:

```
firstLetters [3] = 'c';
```

bearing in mind that the first character is at index zero.

To change the value stored in `holder`'s second location to `10`, we could write:

```
holder[1] = 10;
```

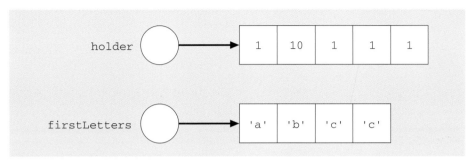

Figure 7   Changing contents of arrays

Of course, if we had a large array, it would not make sense to write a statement like this for each element in the array. Later we shall see another way in which you can initialize elements in an array, using what we call *iteration*.

Just as we saw with strings (and it is true of all references), we can make an array reference variable refer to a different object. If we write:

```
int [] holder2 = {1, 2, 3};
holder = holder2;
```

then we will obtain the result as shown in Figure 8.

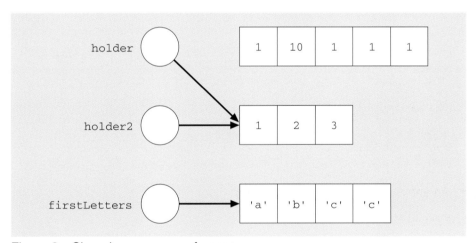

Figure 8   Changing an array reference

The result is that a new array is created, and the old array is no longer referenced by the variable `holder`.

6.2 Accessing array data

As before, we can refer to an item using the index enclosed in square brackets after the name of the array. For example, the fragment of code shown below adds the second and third items in the array `holder` and places the result in the `int` variable `result`.

```
int i = 1;
int result;
result = holder[i] + holder[i + 1];
```

(After this, `result` holds the value 5, obtained by adding 2 + 3.)

We can also use the array data to update itself or another array:

```
holder[1] = holder[1] * holder[2]; // Figure 9
```

The meaning of this is that the array values at indexes 1 and 2 are accessed and multiplied, to give 6. This value is then stored at index 1. The result is shown in Figure 9.

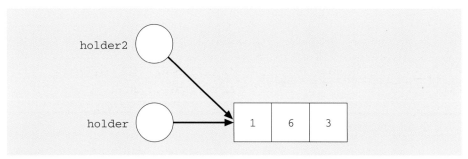

Figure 9   After assigning **holder[1] * holder[2]** to **holder[1]**

6.3 The array instance variable `length`

It is important that we do not accidentally attempt to access an array element beyond the array's capacity, as this will give a run-time error. Arrays have an instance variable `length`, which gives the capacity of the array. The expression:

```
firstLetters.length
```

represents the number of locations in the array `firstLetters`.

Note that a dot is used to refer to the instance variable.

Pitfalls with using `length`

You will have seen the expression:

```
holder.length
```

Activity 2.5
Using arrays.

which gives the number of elements in the array `holder` and you might have wondered why it was different to the use of `length` with strings, as in:

```
name.length();
```

`holder[holder. length -1]` refers to the last element in the array.

where `name` references a `String`. The answer is that `length` is an instance variable associated with arrays, while `length()` is a method associated with strings. This is an unfortunate inconsistency in the Java language.

Don't worry if you can't remember which of string and array has a `length()` method. The compiler will remind you! What is more important is that you try to write code that will continue to work even if your array or string variable references change.

It is also important to bear in mind that array `length` will give the number of locations in an array, not the number of initialized locations.

SAQ 10

What is wrong with each of the following array-initializing expressions?

(a) `int [] f = { true, false};`

(b) `char [] chara = { "c", "d", "e"};`

(c) `boolean b [] = { FALSE, TRUE, FALSE};`

ANSWERS ....

(a) The values `true` and `false` are not compatible with the integer type.

(b) The characters should be in single quotes:

```
char [] chara = {'c', 'd', 'e'};
```

(c) The boolean literals are `false` and `true`, not `FALSE` and `TRUE`.

6.4 Mutability of strings and arrays

Arrays and strings are both fixed-length entities: they cannot be extended or even shrunk.

We can write:

```
int [] holder = { 1, 1, 1, 1, 1 };
int [] holder2 = { 1, 2, 3 };
holder = holder2; // doesn't change first array
```

However, as we illustrated in Figure 8, the third line above does not change the length of the original array referenced by `holder` (with all 1s in it). It makes `holder` reference a different array of smaller length (which is also referenced by `holder2`). Any array length is fixed at the point when the array is created. (The contents of the array can be changed, provided we have a reference to the array.)

Similarly, we can write:

```
String s = "fish";
s = "wonderbread";
```

and this does not change the length of the original string, `"fish"`. What changes is the reference `s`, which at first points to a `String` object with value `"fish"`, and then subsequently points to a different `String` object with value `"wonderbread"`.

Whereas contents of arrays can be changed, contents of strings cannot. Strings are said to be **immutable**: they cannot be changed at all, once created.

There is a more flexible type for manipulating sequences of characters, called `StringBuffer`.

7 Repetitive processing

All programming languages allow sections of code to be executed repeatedly while some condition is satisfied. This powerful facility is often called **iteration**. For example, this enables the contents of an array of integers to be summed without writing out an expression involving every element of the array. In this section we discuss two important Java flow control structures for repetitive processing: the while and for statements.

7.1 The while statement

There is a variation called do ... while, which we do not consider here.

The first iteration facility that we will introduce is the while statement. This has the general form:

```
while (logical_expression)
{
    statements;
}
```

The semantics of the while statement are as follows.

> While the *logical_expression* is true, the *statements* are executed. The truth of the *logical_expression* is rechecked after each execution of the body of the while.

A very simple example of the use of the while statement is shown below:

As usual, we indent the code to increase readability.

```
int [ ] vals = {10,20,30,40,50};
int i = 0, sum = 0;
while (i < 3)
{
    sum = sum + vals [i];
    i++;
}
```

This simple piece of code first creates an array and two integer variables. The body of the while adds the ith element of the array vals to the value stored in the variable sum; after this it increments the variable i used to index the array. The effect of the code is to add to sum the first three elements of the array vals.

SAQ 11

Is this statement true or false? "The code in the body of a while loop is executed at least once."

ANSWER..

False: it can be executed zero, one or more times.

7.2 The **for** statement

Another important statement to implement repetitive processing in Java is the `for` statement. The general form of this statement is:

```
for (control_initializer; logical_expression;
    control_adjustment)
{
    statements;
}
```

Later in the course you will meet another version of the `for` statement, the for-each statement.

The *statements* are executed repeatedly under the control of a variable, referred to as the control variable. The semantics of the `for` statement are as follows.

The control variable is created and given its initial value in *control_initializer*. Next, the *logical_expression* determines if the loop body is executed. After each time the *statements* are executed, *control_adjustment* defines the new value of the control variable, and the *logical_expression* is checked again. The loop terminates when the *logical_expression* becomes `false`.

The *control_initializer* is only executed once and is the first statement to be executed by the `for` loop.

Comparing the general form of the `for` statement with that of the `while` statement, it is clear that they contain the same elements but that these are arranged differently.

Example 5

An example of the use of the `for` statement, which could be used to initialize or change elements of an array, is shown below:

```
int [] a = {1,2,3,4,5,6,7,8,9,10};
for (int i = 0; i < a.length; i++)
{
    a [i] = 10;
}
```

The scope of `i` here is the body of the `for` loop.

Here the statement `a [i] = 10;` is repeatedly executed. To begin with, the value of i is zero (`int i= 0` corresponds to *control_initializer*). Then the test i `< a.length` is performed. As this is true, the loop body `a [i] = 10` is executed, in this case resulting in `a [0]` being assigned the value 10. Next, i is incremented by one (`i++` corresponds to *control_adjustment*).

Then *logical_expression* is evaluated again. Because it is `true`, we repeat the execution of `a [i] = 10`, in this case resulting in `a [1]` being assigned the value 10, and increment i again. This process is repeated until i equals the length of the array, when the condition `10 < a.length` is false, meaning that the statement `a [i] = 10` is not executed, and the loop ends. (Remember that the last element of this array will be `a [9]`, so each array location has been initialized to 10 after this loop.)

Example 6

The expressions used in each part of the `for` control structure can be more complex, as in the following:

```
for (int i = 2 * start; i <= endValue; i = i + 2)
{
    statements;
}
```

This loop executes *statements* as long as the condition `i <= endValue` is true. Initially, the control variable `i` has the value `2 * start`, and if the condition is true we execute *statements*. Then the control variable is incremented by two each time the loop body is executed. This continues until the value of `i` is greater than the contents of the variable `endValue`.

A `for` statement can always be rewritten as a `while` statement, but sometimes one or the other is more readable. A `for` statement is generally used when a fixed number of iterations is required, as in our first example above. A `while` loop is often preferred where the looping condition is complex.

SAQ 12

Explain why, in Example 5, the condition we used was `i < a.length` and not `i <= a.length`.

ANSWER..

This is because the first index of the array is zero, and the last is the array's capacity minus one. Therefore we should not allow `i` to reach `a`'s capacity (which is `a.length`). If we did, we would be indexing off the end of the array and a run-time error would occur.

SAQ 13

Write fragments of code to do the following using a `for` loop.

(a) Print out the squares of the numbers 1 to 20 inclusive, in ascending order, with some explanatory text.

(b) Print the characters of the English alphabet in reverse order from `'z'` to `'a'`, with some explanatory text. Hint: you can do arithmetic with `char` variables, because their underlying type is integral.

ANSWERS ....

There are variations possible on the following sample answers. In all cases, the control variable name could be varied.

(a)

```
for (int j = 1; j <= 20; j++)
{
    System.out.println(j + " squared = " + j * j);
}
```

(b)

```
System.out.println("The alphabet in reverse:");
for (char ch = 'z'; ch >= 'a'; ch--)
{
    System.out.println(ch);
}
```

You can use the decrement operator on a `char`, because its underlying type is integral.

Activity 2.6
Experimenting with `for` loops.

Activity 2.7
Using `for` loops with data stored in arrays.

8 Developing some methods

In this section you will study two examples to give you more practice with writing methods. The methods will use the Java flow control structures for iteration and conditional processing and the array data structure.

8.1 Example 1: a bag

A **bag**, as shown in Figure 10, is a collection of data that keeps track of the number of times an item is contained in it.

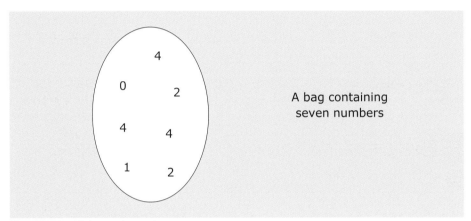

Figure 10   A bag of numbers

This example shows the code for methods associated with a simple bag that keeps track of the number of times the integers ranging from 0 to 9 are stored in it. We show two methods:

▶ a method that adds an integer to a bag, addToBag;

▶ a method that returns the number of occurrences of a particular integer within a bag, findNum.

We will assume that all the arguments passed to the methods will be in the range 0 to 9, so that we do not have to check that these arguments are valid.

A natural way of storing the items in this bag would be an array that has 10 locations corresponding to the 10 possible integers that it could contain. We will assume that this instance variable will have the name bagVals:

```
int [ ] bagVals = {0,0,0,0,0,0,0,0,0,0}
```

By initializing the array locations to zero we are indicating that the bag is empty: there are no occurrences of any of the integers. In practice, a method to initialize the bagVals array might be a useful thing, allowing us to start our bag from an empty state.

The code for the method addToBag is shown below. It takes one argument, which is the integer to be added. (This integer must be in the range 0 to 9.)

```
public void addToBag (int toBeAdded)
{
    ++bagVals [toBeAdded];
}
```

Thus, the *n*th array location contains the number of times that the value *n* has been added to the bag. For example, if this method were called with the argument 1, then `bagVals [1]` would be incremented from 0 to 1. If this were to happen a second time, `bagVals [1]` would be incremented from 1 to 2. The following method would have the same effect:

```
public void addToBag (int toBeAdded)
{
    bagVals [toBeAdded] = bagVals [toBeAdded] + 1;
}
```

The code for the method that returns the number of occurrences of a particular integer within a bag is shown below. It has one argument, the integer whose number of occurrences we want to know.

```
public int findNum (int lookedFor)
{
    return bagVals [lookedFor];
}
```

For example, if the argument `lookedFor` is 1, then we return the value stored in `bagVals [1]`.

Remember that the keyword `public` specifies that any other class can use this method and the keyword `int` indicates that an integer value is returned from the method.

Activity 2.8
Adding methods to the `Bag` class.

8.2 Example 2: a collection of computer names

In this example, we develop a set of methods for an object that contains a collection of computer names. Each name in the collection represents a computer currently connected to a network.

There will be two instance variables associated with this object: `computers`, which is an array of strings storing the names of computers, and `numConnected`, which is an integer variable that contains the current number of computers connected together in the network. We shall not worry about the declaration of these instance variables now, but concentrate on the methods. We shall assume that four methods are required:

▶ a method that returns the number of computers in the network, `getNumConnected`;

▶ a method that adds a named computer to the network, `addComputer`;

▶ a method that returns the index at which a named computer is found in the collection or –1 if the computer is not found in the collection, `indexOf`;

▶ a method that removes a named computer from the network, `removeComputer`.

In developing the code, we will make simplifying assumptions:

▶ we will not be adding a computer with a name that is the same as a computer already in the network;

▶ we will always have enough room in the `computers` array to hold all the computers we want to add to the network.

The first method returns the number of computers:

```
public int getNumConnected ()
{
    return numConnected;
}
```

The method that adds a computer name to the collection of computers is shown below. The instance variable `numConnected` is serving two purposes: it is the number of computers in our collection and also marks the next unoccupied location in the `computers` array (we fill the array from the lowest index upwards). We are assuming that `numConnected` will be initialized to 0 to begin with, so that we fill the array correctly.

```
public void addComputer (String addedComputer)
{
    computers [numConnected] = addedComputer;
    numConnected++;
}
```

A sketch of the system after adding the computer named `"fifi"` to the collection by invoking `addComputer("fifi")` is shown in Figure 11.

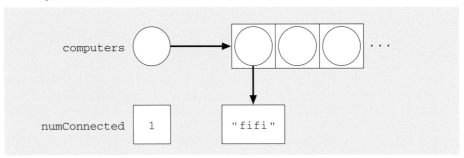

Figure 11   After adding `"fifi"` to the collection, the next place to be filled in the array is at index 1

A method, `indexOf`, that returns the index of a named computer in the network, or –1 if the computer is not found, is shown below.

This method makes use of a method of `String` objects that you have not yet seen, called `equals`. The `equals` method returns `true` if two strings contain the same characters, and otherwise it returns `false`.

So the expression `wantedComputer.equals(computers [i])` returns true if the string referenced by `computers [i]` and the string referenced by `wantedComputer` contain the same characters. If we had written `computers [i].equals(wantedComputer)` the result would be the same. In the first case, the method would be invoked on the object referenced by `wantedComputer`, and in the second on the object referenced by `computers [i]`, but the result returned is the same.

```
public int indexOf (String wantedComputer)
{
    boolean found = false;
    int i = 0;
    while (!found && i < numConnected)
    {
        found = wantedComputer.equals(computers [i]);
        i++;
    }
    if (found)
    {
        // i was incremented after the find
        return i - 1;
    }
    else
    {
        return -1;
    }
}
```

The final method, `removeComputer`, removes a computer from the network. This is achieved by finding the point in the array where the computer name is stored and then shifting down each name that lies after it.

```
public void removeComputer (String unwantedComputer)
{
    // find the index of the computer
    int i = indexOf(unwantedComputer);
    // if it is not -1, the computer was found
    if (i > -1)
    {
        /*  Move the computers after this position to the left by one.
            The body of this loop is not executed if the computer
            is last in the collection. */
        for (int j = i; j < numConnected - 1; j++)
        {
            computers [j] = computers [j + 1];
        }
        numConnected--;
    }
}
```

This method does not alter the value stored in the position last filled in the array, but because `numConnected` is decremented, that value will not be considered part of the collection. It will be overwritten if another computer is added to the collection.

The code for these methods can now be used in any program. For example, the fragment of code below adds a computer called `"Pentium200"` to a collection of computers referenced by `localComputers`, then removes the computer `"Vroom486"` and finally places in the integer variable `collCount` the current number of computers in the collection.

```
localComputers.addComputer("Pentium200");
localComputers.removeComputer("Vroom486");
int collCount = localComputers.getNumConnected();
```

Again, notice the format of the expressions, which all involve methods being invoked on objects. Notice the lack of arguments in the third method, which does not require them.

Activity 2.9
Adding methods to the computer collection class.

9 Strings and arrays revisited

To conclude this unit we are returning to strings and arrays. We feel that before reading the next unit it would be useful for you to see more examples of object methods being invoked. Also, whilst strings and arrays are objects, we want to point out that we have been creating them using shortcut mechanisms that are not generally available to objects. This also will help to prepare you for the next unit, because other objects you will encounter from now on cannot be created by assignment of a literal (as we did with strings) or by using an initializer (as we did with arrays).

Remember that with reference types, there are several steps taken to create a useful object, referenced by a variable:

▶ declaration of a reference variable of the appropriate type;

▶ creation (and initialization) of an object of the chosen type;

▶ making the reference variable refer to the created object.

For example, the declaration:

```
String fileName;
```

declares a string reference called `fileName`, but does not create an object. We saw earlier that we can make a string reference refer to an initialized object by means of an assignment. For example:

```
fileName = "Tdata.txt";
```

sets the reference `fileName` to refer to the string object containing the characters `"Tdata.txt"`. Most objects cannot be created by literals like this.

9.1 The `StringBuffer` type

A more typical class type in Java, in terms of object creation, is `StringBuffer`, which can be used to handle sequences of characters. A `StringBuffer` object is *mutable*: it can be changed once it has been created.

However, to create a `StringBuffer` object we cannot simply write a string literal. The following would be illegal:

```
StringBuffer userName;
userName = "Jones21";  // illegal!
```

The reason is that the expression on the right-hand side of this assignment is a `String`, and we are trying to assign it to a reference variable of a different type, `StringBuffer`.

To make a `StringBuffer` object, we require a completely different syntax:

```
new StringBuffer("Jones21")
```

This uses the keyword `new` with the type of the object being created (`StringBuffer`) and an argument (`"Jones21"`, in this case) that allows initialization of the object. For the time being, do not worry too much about this syntax. We shall return to discuss it in detail in *Unit 3*.

Normally you would write such an expression on the right-hand side of an assignment, as follows:

```
StringBuffer userName;
userName = new StringBuffer("Jones21");
```

The first line here creates the reference variable, while the second makes the reference refer to a `StringBuffer` object.

Why is there different syntax to create a `String` and a `StringBuffer`? The answer is that creating strings is a common task and so Java provides the shortcut we have been using. This is a special feature provided for strings!

However, a `String` is an object and all objects can be created in the manner used for `StringBuffer` above: using the keyword `new`, the name of the type and some initializing data. In this case, we can write:

```
String filename;
/* create string using new */
filename = new String("Tdata.txt");
```

We do not advise you to create strings in this way.

9.2 Array creation with `new`

We hinted before that our method for creating arrays, using array initializers, was limited. We used syntax like the following:

```
int [ ] myArray = {1,2,1,2};
```

The above example creates an array of four integers, initialized to the values 1, 2, 1 and 2; the reference variable `myArray` is initialized to reference this array.

You would not want to create a large array this way, because you would have to list values for all the elements in the array individually.

All array types in Java are reference types, not primitives. As such, array objects also can be created using the `new` keyword. We could create an array with room for four `int` values as follows:

```
new int [4]
```

This expression is similar to `new StringBuffer("text")` in that it uses the word `new`, the type of the thing we want to create (`int[]`) and an argument (4). It is different in that it uses square brackets instead of parentheses around the argument.

This is a special syntax used just for arrays. All other objects use the parentheses syntax.

To make an array reference refer to an array object we now have an alternative syntax. For example, we can write:

```
int [ ] myArray = new int [4];
```

Unlike when we used an array initializer, we have not stated what the elements in this array are. We have only stated that there should be room for four integers to be stored. We can initialize these elements (they will default to the value 0) using assignment to individual locations:

```
myArray [0] - 1;
myArray [1] = 2;
myArray [2] = 1;
myArray [3] = 2;
```

This is equivalent to the following:

```
int [ ] myArray = {1,2,1,2} ;
```

The significance is that we now have syntax to create arrays of larger dimensions simply:

```
int [ ] myArray = new int [400];
```

Using an array initializer in this case would be hard to read and write, at the very least.

We can still initialize elements of such an array, but we would be unlikely to do it by writing one assignment for each location. Instead, we would use iteration.

9.3 | More string methods

A list of some frequently used `String` methods is shown in Table 5.

Table 5 Some **String** methods

A receiver object is the object on which a method is invoked. For example in `myString.equals (str)`, `myString` is the receiver string object.

Method	Meaning	Returns
equals(str)	returns `true` if the passed `String str` has the same characters as the receiver string object	a `boolean`
length()	returns the number of characters in a `String`	an `int`
charAt(i)	returns the character at the `int` index i in the `String`; the index begins at zero	a `char` (It is an error if i is out of range.)
indexOf(str)	returns the starting index of the string `str` within the receiver object, or –1 if not found	an `int`
substring(int1, int2)	returns the substring of the receiver string, starting at `int1` and finishing at `int2 – 1`	a `String` (It is an error if the indexes are out of range.)

Notice that the `length` method does not require any arguments. All the examples above return a value, but this is not a requirement of methods in general.

SAQ 14

What is wrong with each of the following statements?

(a) `char ch = new char [5] ;`

(b) `Boolean [ ] b = new boolean [3] ;`

(c) `int [ ] f = new int [–1] ;`

(d) `int [ ] byte = new int [10] ;`

(e) `char [ ] ch = char [5] ;`

(f) `boolean b [ ] = new boolean [ ] ;`

ANSWERS ....

(a) The type of the left-hand side of the assignment is not an array of characters. This declaration is missing square brackets. It should read:

```
char [ ] ch = new char [5] ;
```

(b) `Boolean` is not the same as `boolean`.

(c) The array size declared cannot be negative.

(d) The name `byte` is a keyword, so it cannot be the name of a variable.

(e) The declaration is missing the keyword `new`.

(f) The declaration has not specified the size of the `boolean` array.

10 Summary

In this unit you have been introduced to the main data types and control structures that are used within Java and we have discussed small pieces of code.

We have distinguished between primitive types and reference types. Variables of a primitive type contain values of their declared type, whilst reference variables are 'pointers' to objects.

We saw that we could convert between most primitive types by the process called casting, although this would sometimes result in loss of some information. Casting between reference and primitive types is not legal.

You have been introduced to the various operators that can be used with the primitive types, and the logical operators for `boolean` types in order to create logical expressions. Even though there are operator precedence rules, it was discussed that bracketing provides a more understandable way of structuring your code.

You have been introduced to flow control structures in Java for conditional processing and repetitive processing. The `if` and `switch` statements give us ways to select whether or not a block of code will be executed, whereas `for` and `while` loops provide a mechanism to repeatedly execute blocks of code.

We saw that an array allows you to create a collection of items of the same type, and facilitates processing them as a collection, allowing us to write relatively compact code. Arrays also have a shortcut initializer syntax. It was discussed that the `for` loop is particularly suitable for iterating through an array.

We discussed strings as an example of a very commonly used reference type. Typically, an object's state can be altered, but we saw that objects of type `String` are immutable, and that the length of an array is fixed on creation.

The `StringBuffer` type provides us with a mutable form of string. The types `String` and `StringBuffer`, as well as all arrays, are reference types in Java, meaning that we create objects of their type and invoke methods on those objects in order to perform processing. You saw examples of objects being created using syntax involving the keyword `new`.

We have noted that there are some shortcut operators associated with strings: string objects can be created using a string literal and we can concatenate strings (and types converted to strings) using the + operator.

Unit 3 will describe the key ideas of an object-oriented programming language and their implementation in Java. We have tried to prepare the ground by devoting some time in this unit to the `StringBuffer` type.

LEARNING OUTCOMES

When you have completed this unit, you should be able to:

► write fragments of code that use the primitive types, arrays and string types in the Java language;

► write code to change the flow of control in programs using `if` and `switch` statements;

► write looping constructs using `while` and `for` loops.

Concepts

The following concepts have been introduced in this unit:

array, array initializer, bag, body, `boolean`, casting, code block, conditional processing, data type, declaration, empty string, escape sequence, expression, floating-point type, flow control structure, immutable, index, initialization, integral type, iterate, iteration, literal, local variable, logical expression, operator, operator precedence, prefix, postfix, primitive type, promotion, reference type, relational operator, scope, selection statement, statement, string, strongly typed language, type, Unicode.

Index